Julia Wall

Adam Nickel

Bruno's Tea

Fast Forward
Silver Level 23

Text: Peter Millett
Illustrations: Adam Nickel
Editor: Cameron Macintosh
Design: Ami Sharpe
Series design: James Lowe
Production controller: Seona Galbally
Audio recordings: Juliet Hill, Picture Start
Spoken by: Matthew King and Abbe Holmes
Reprint: Siew Han Ong

Text © 2007 Cengage Learning Australia Pty Limited
Illustrations © 2007 Cengage Learning Australia Pty Limited

Copyright Notice
This Work is copyright. No part of this Work may be reproduced, stored in a retrieval system, or transmitted in any form or by any means without prior written permission of the Publisher. Except as permitted under the *Copyright Act 1968*, for example any fair dealing for the purposes of private study, research, criticism or review, subject to certain limitations. These limitations include: Restricting the copying to a maximum of one chapter or 10% of this book, whichever is greater; Providing an appropriate notice and warning with the copies of the Work disseminated; Taking all reasonable steps to limit access to these copies to people authorised to receive these copies; Ensuring you hold the appropriate Licences issued by the Copyright Agency Limited ("CAL"), supply a remuneration notice to CAL and pay any required fees.

ISBN 978 0 17 012694 6
ISBN 978 0 17 012693 9 (set)

Cengage Learning Australia
Level 7, 80 Dorcas Street
South Melbourne, Victoria Australia 3205
Phone: 1300 790 853

Cengage Learning New Zealand
Unit 4B Rosedale Office Park
331 Rosedale Road, Albany, North Shore NZ 0632
Phone: 0800 449 725

For learning solutions, visit **cengage.com.au**

Printed in Australia by Ligare Pty Ltd
6 7 8 9 10 11 20 19 18 17 16

Evaluated in independent research by staff from the Department of Language, Literacy and Arts Education at the University of Melbourne.

Bruno's Tea

Julia Wall
Adam Nickel

Contents

Chapter 1 **Mr Green's Order**   4
Chapter 2 **Going Inside**   12
Chapter 3 **The Mystery Explained**   16
Chapter 4 **Talking to Dad**   20

Chapter 1

Mr Green's Order

"Here's the shopping for Mr Green,"
said Dad,
handing me a big plastic bag.

Dad owned a milk bar,
and sometimes I helped out
after school with deliveries.
We had our regulars,
but times were hard.
Dad said it was the home deliveries
that kept us in business –
that, and the tea Dad imported
from Fuzhou.
Dad was well-known for his tea,
and people came from miles around
to buy it.

Mr Green's Order

I loaded up my bicycle with
Mr Green's shopping.
His order always included
three packets of Dad's tea.
How Mr Green could drink that much
each week was a mystery to me.

"See you later, Chen," said Dad.
He always called me by
my Chinese name.
Dad's parents came from China
in the 1950s.
I had a yuan coin they brought
with them.

Mr Green's Order

I cycled out into the sun,
wishing I could drive –
it would be so much quicker
to make deliveries.
Dad always said the exercise
was good for me.
I knew he was right,
but I'd already decided
that when I left home,
the first thing I would do
was buy a car.

I loved anything to do with cars,
and I'd decided
I would be a mechanic,
although I knew it wasn't
what Dad had in mind for me.
He'd already started saying
to his friends,
"When Chen goes to university …"
If that happened, I would be the first
person in my family to go,
and it would be
a great honour for my dad.
But it wasn't what I wanted.

Mr Green's Order

I stopped outside Mr Green's house,
looking for Bruno, his dog.
He wasn't out the front like usual.
I knocked on Mr Green's door.
"Mr Green?" I called out.
There was no reply.

Bruno's Tea

I decided to leave Mr Green's order
by the back door,
which was what I did if a customer
wasn't at home.
I walked through Mr Green's lawn.
It was usually high, and this day
it was up to my knees.

Mr Green's Order

Bruno wasn't out the back either.
Something wasn't right –
I just knew it.
Dad always said not to go inside
a customer's house
unless I'm invited, but I had to
find out what was happening.
I went back around the front,
and gave the door a push.

It was open.
I took a deep breath,
and stepped into Mr Green's hall.

Chapter 2

Going Inside

I'd never been inside
Mr Green's house before.
Usually I handed him his shopping,
and that was that.
If Dad could see me now,
he'd be furious.

I looked into each room,
calling Mr Green's name as I went.
The last thing I wanted was to give us
both a fright.
As I went through the house,
I noticed he was into cars.
Each room was filled with stuff like
old tyres and radiators.

I finished searching the house
and decided there was nothing more
I could do.
But something was still telling me
that Mr Green was in trouble.
I walked back through the grass
and past his garage,
thinking about what to do next.
That was when I heard a whimper.
Bruno!

I stopped outside the garage.
I felt scared to go in –
scared of Bruno,
and scared of what I might find.
From outside, I could see two cars.
There were car parts
and tools everywhere.

Chapter 3
The Mystery Explained

I heard Bruno's whimper again.
It was coming from the back
of the garage.
I moved slowly inside,
watching where I put my feet.

The Mystery Explained

Bruno came up to me
and pulled on my shorts.
He didn't bark at me
like he usually did.
I could see a shoe near the front
of one of the cars.
"Mr Green," I said, moving closer.
"It's me, Chen."

Bruno's Tea

Mr Green opened his eyes and sat up.
He told me he'd been working
on one of his cars,
when he tripped and hurt his ankle.
He was in so much pain he could
hardly move.
I was glad I'd heard Bruno's whimper.
If I hadn't come along when I did ...

I helped Mr Green to his feet,
upsetting a bowl of brown liquid
onto the floor.
"Sorry, Mr Green," I said.
"Was that petrol?"

The Mystery Explained

"No," Mr Green laughed.
"It's your dad's tea.
Bruno loves it, so I always make him
a bowl.
Just as well, or he'd be dead
in this heat."
That explained the three packets
a week!
I helped Mr Green inside
so that he could phone his sister
to take him to the doctor.

Chapter 4

Talking to Dad

Mr Green was so grateful,
he gave me a big reward.
Dad even put a sign next to his tea:
"Good for Animals, Too!"

That week, Dad's sales went up.
Dad was so pleased with me that
I decided now would be the best time
to talk about my plans.

"Dad," I said.

"Yes, Chen?"
Dad didn't look up
from drinking his tea
and reading his Chinese newspaper.
He'd just started importing them,
and they were really popular.

I took a deep breath and wished
I couldn't hear the blood
pounding in my ears.
"Dad, I've decided I don't want to go
to university.
I want to be a mechanic."
The words came out in a rush.

Dad put his tea down slowly
and looked at me.
"Chen," he said, "you have to do
what's right for you.
My parents wanted me to be
a market gardener,
but I told them I wanted
to sell things, not grow them."
Dad took a big mouthful of tea.
"Is this what you really want,
this car thing?"

I nodded. "It is, Dad.
I've thought about it a lot."

"Then I'll do everything I can to help,"
Dad said.

Talking to Dad

My heart stopped pounding,
and I felt light.
"Thanks, Dad."

Dad and I didn't show a lot
of affection,
but right then I gave him
the biggest hug I'd ever given him.

Then, I loaded up my bicycle
with Mr Green's shopping.
He was going to show me the car
he was working on.
As always, his order included three
packets of Bruno's tea.